DISCOVERING MAPS AND GLOBES

WRITTEN BY REBECCA STARK
COVER ILLUSTRATED BY KORYN AGNELLO
TEXT ILLUSTRATED BY KORYN AGNELLO & KAREN SIGLER

ISBN 1-56644-036-X

© 1999 Educational Impressions, Inc., Hawthorne, NJ

Printed in the U.S.A.

TABLE OF CONTENTS

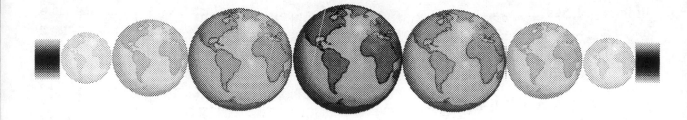

OTHER BOOKS BY REBECCA STARK:

Birds (Book and Poster)
Our Environment (Book and Poster)
The Middle Ages (Book and Poster)
Native American Cultures (Book and Poster)
Weather (Book and Poster)
I've Got Another Idea
What Would You Do?
" -OLOGIES" SERIES
    Archaeology
    Mythology
    Anthropology
    Psychology
CREATIVE VENTURES SERIES
    Mysteries and UFOs
    Ancient Civilizations
    The Future
    The Media
"FROM THE FIRST DAY OF SCHOOL TO THE LAST" SERIES
    September
    October
    November
    December
    January
    February
    March
    April
    May and June (with activities for the summer months)

INTRODUCTION
TO THE TEACHER

Make your students' world a little smaller and a lot more interesting with this comprehensive unit on maps and globes. Activities build important geography and social studies skills; they also encourage critical and creative thinking. The first three activities—All Kinds of Maps, Map Match, and Fill in the Blank— can be useful in assessing how much your students already know about maps and globes. The last two activities—Discovering Maps and Globes Crossword and What's the Question?—can serve as tool to evaluate your students' knowledge at the completion of the unit. (What's the Question? is a Jeopardy-type quiz game.)

Discovering Maps and Globes teaches students important social studies concepts. Children are introduced to all kinds of maps: political maps, physical maps, product maps, weather maps, and others. They learn the language and terms necessary to understand and to use maps and globes effectively. Longitude and latitude are studied in depth. Longitude's relation to time zones and latitude's relationship to climate are presented.

All Kinds of Maps

Maps are flat pictures of places. There are many types of maps. Each provides us with different kinds of information. Brainstorm and think of many different types of maps. The list has been started for you.

Treasure maps

Map Match

Match the map type on the left with the description on the right. You may want to use your dictionary.

___ 1. atlas

___ 2. historical map

___ 3. physical map

___ 4. political map

___ 5. population map

___ 6. precipitation map

___ 7. product map

___ 8. relief map

___ 9. road map

___ 10. street map

___ 11. undersea map

___ 12. weather map

A. Shows land configuration with contour lines, colors, or shading; may be raised.

B. Shows the forecasted weather in a particular area.

C. Shows where people live in an area and/or how many people live there.

D. Gives us a picture of events in an area at particular times in history.

E. A book of maps.

F. Shows an area's natural resources.

G. Shows roads and highways; helps us drive from one place to another.

H. Shows rivers, lakes, mountains, and other such features.

I. Shows the depth of the ocean in an area; also called a chart.

J. Shows boundaries, such as those between states and countries.

K. Shows the amount of rain, snow, and hail that falls in an area.

L. Includes all the streets in a town or neighborhood.

Fill in the Blanks

In order to use maps effectively, it is important to understand some basic concepts and terms. Choose from the words in the box to fill in the blanks.

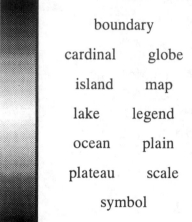

boundary

cardinal   globe

island   map

lake   legend

ocean   plain

plateau   scale

symbol

1. The northern _____ of the United States is Canada.

2. A(n) _____ is a large inland body of fresh or salt water.

3. A(n) _____ is a list of symbols on a map.

4. East is one of the four _____ points on a compass.

5. A(n) _____ is used to show the relative distance on a map.

6. The representation of the earth in the shape of a sphere is a(n) _____.

7. The _____ is the body of salt water that covers about 72% of the earth.

8. A written sign or mark used to represent something else is a(n) _____.

9. Land surrounded by water is a(n) _____.

10. A(n) _____ is an extensive, level, usually treeless stretch of land.

11. A raised, relatively level stretch of land is a(n) _____.

12. The representation of the earth on a flat surface is a(n) _____.

Directions

In order to read a map, it is necessary to understand the four cardinal, or principal, directions: north (N), south (S), east (E), and west (W). On most maps north is at the top and south is at the bottom. East would then be in the direction of the right side of the map, and west would be in the direction of the left side of the map.

By combining the four cardinal directions, we get four more directions: northeast (NE), southeast (SE), northwest (NW), and southwest (SW).

Fill in the missing points on the compass. Use the letter abbreviations for those directions.

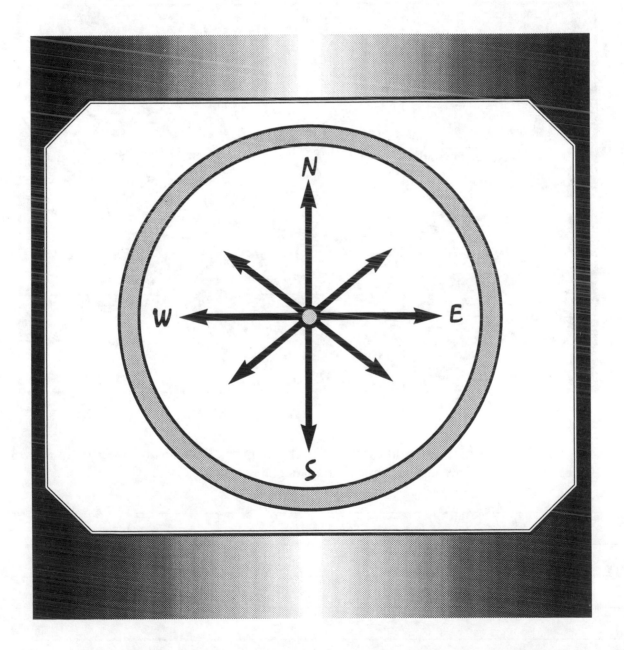

Using Grids

Many maps have grids to help us find places. For example, this map gives each city a number and a letter; this information tells us where the city is on the map.

Study the map. Without reading the information below the map, look for Alpine.

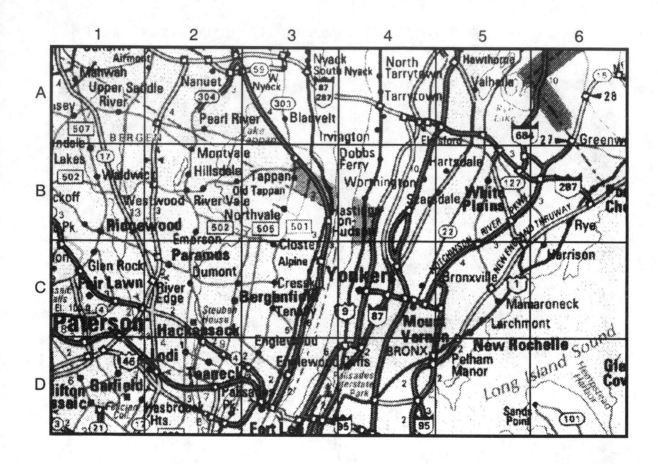

Alpine is at C-3. "C" means it is in Column C. The number "3" means it is located in Row 3. Did this information help you find Alpine? Explain.

_____

_____

_____

_____

_____

Scale

Maps come in many sizes. Without a map scale it would be difficult to judge distance accurately. A map scale tells us how many miles (or kilometers) each inch (or meter) represents.

According to the scale on this map, one inch equals ten miles.

POINT A •

•POINT C

•POINT D

•POINT B

SCALE: ‾‾‾‾‾(one inch)‾‾‾‾‾ = 10 miles

Measure the distance between Point A and Point B.
Point A and Point B are _____ inches apart; therefore, those two places are _____ miles apart.

Measure the distance between Point C and Point D.
Point C and Point D are _____ inches apart; therefore, those two places are _____ miles apart.

Measure the distance between Point A and Point D.
Point A and Point D are _____ inches apart; therefore, those two places are _____ miles apart.

How Far Away Is It?

Using the scale on a map, we can figure out the distance between two places. The map below shows a portion of southern New Jersey. On this map one inch equals eight miles.

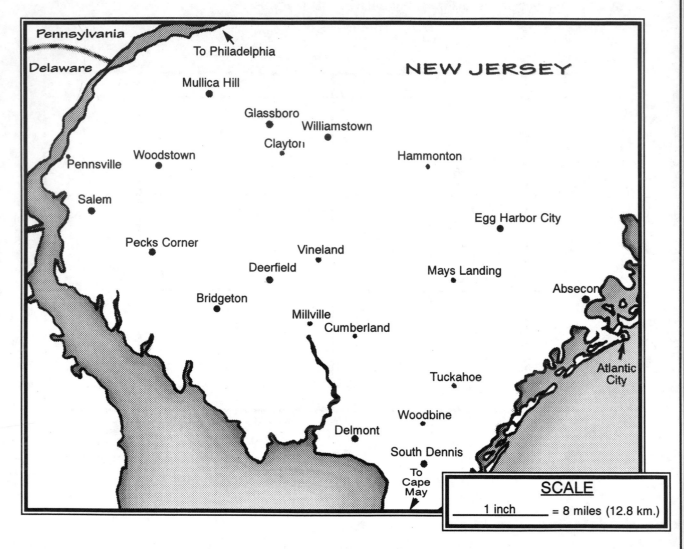

Use the scale to figure out the distances between the following towns:

1. Delmont to South Dennis   _____

2. Bridgeton to Salem   _____

3. Woodstown to Mullica Hill   _____

4. Pecks Corner to Deerfield   _____

5. Egg Harbor City to Absecon   _____

6. Glassboro to Williamstown   _____

Legends

On many maps, usually near the scale, you will find a group of symbols called a legend. Sometimes this group of symbols is called a key. The symbols are not the same for all maps!

On the left are some commonly used symbols. See if you can match them to the types of places they represent.

___ 1.   A. Airport

___ 2.   B. Picnic Area

___ 3.   C. Park or Recreation Area

___ 4.   D. Mountains

___ 5.   E. Beach

___ 6.   F. Railroad

___ 7.   G. River

___ 8.   H. Lake

JUST FOR FUN: Design symbols that might be used to represent each of the following places.

FOREST   BIRD SANCTUARY

AMUSEMENT PARK   ZOOLOGICAL PARK

BUS STATION   UNIVERSITY

C-A-R-T-O-G-R-A-P-H-E-R

A person who makes maps and charts is called a cartographer. See how many words of three or more letters you can form by using the letters in the word "cartographer."

CHALLENGE: I found over 100! Can you find some that I missed?

C-A-R-T-O-G-R-A-P-H-E-R

Road Maps

By looking at the lines representing a road or highway and the shape in which the highway number is enclosed, we can tell the type of road it is.

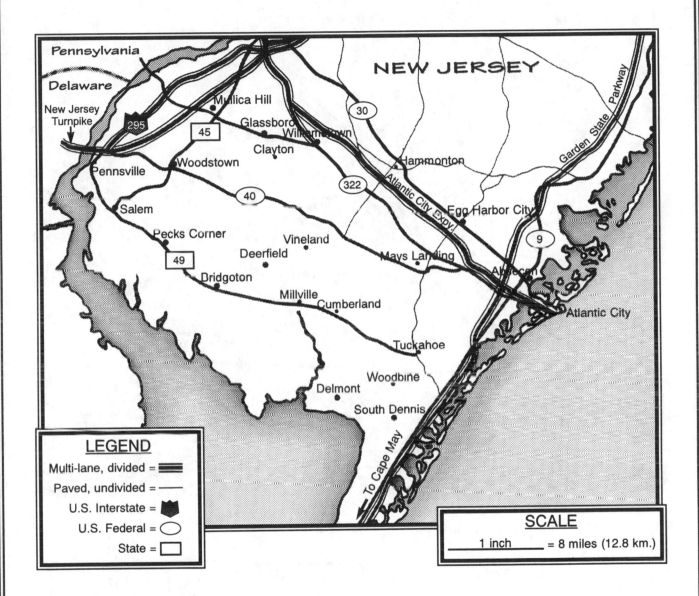

LEGEND
Multi-lane, divided = ▬
Paved, undivided = —
U.S. Interstate = ▰
U.S. Federal = ◯
State = ▢

SCALE
1 inch = 8 miles (12.8 km.)

Use the legend to answer the following questions:

1. Name the interstate highway(s). _____

2. Name the U.S. federal highway(s). _____

3. Name the state highway(s). _____

4. Which is (are) a multi-laned divided highway? _____

Weather Maps

Weather maps have special symbols. This map shows three kinds of fronts: cold, warm, and stationary. It also shows four kinds of weather conditions: rain, thunderstorms, snow, and ice. Temperature bands are shown by varying degrees of shading.

Note: Temperatures are given in degrees Fahrenheit.

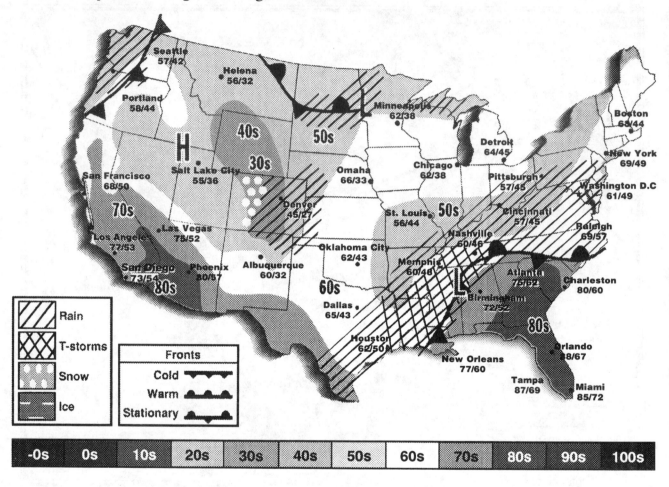

Create your own symbols for the following conditions:

Hail

Cloudy

Tornado
Warning

Sunny

Partly
Cloudy

Windy

Using the weather map on the previous page, answer the following questions:

1. What will the weather be like for Washington, D.C.? What are the expected high and low temperatures?

_____

_____

2. Which of the following cities are expected to have a high temperature in the 80's: Denver, San Diego, Phoenix, Birmingham, Orlando, or Houston?

_____

_____

3. Which area is expected to experience thunderstorms? Which is expecting snow?

_____

_____

4. Which city is expecting the lowest temperature of all those shown on the map? What is that temperature?

_____

_____

5. Are any areas expecting icy conditions?

_____

_____

6. Which type of front is headed for Seattle, Washington? Which type of front is over the northern Great Plains?

_____

_____

7. Which of these cities does not expect rain: Raleigh, New York, Boston, or Cincinatti?

_____

_____

8. Which city expects both a higher high and a lower low temperature than New Orleans?

_____

_____

Colorful Information

Physical maps show us such things as land masses, bodies of water, plains, plateaus, mountains, forests, and deserts. Color is often used to give us special information. The colors used on maps are not always the same.

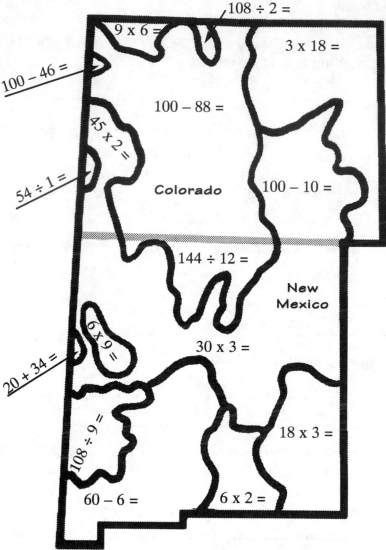

For this activity smooth areas of land, called **plains,** will be shown in green.
Mountains will be shown in brown.
Plateaus, or elevated stretches of level land, will be shown in orange.

In order to know which colors to use you will first have to figure out the math problems. Use the following code to color in the areas:

BROWN (MOUNTAINS) = 12
ORANGE (PLATEAUS) = 90
GREEN (PLAINS) = 54

The Continents

The largest bodies of land are the seven continents: Africa, Antarctica, Asia, Australia, Europe, North America, and South America. Use a world map to help you answer the following questions about the continents.

1. Which continent is bordered on the west by the North Pacific Ocean?

_____

2. Which North American country borders the United States to the south?

_____

3. Which continents are islands?

_____

4. Which continent is separated from Europe by the Ural Mountains?

_____

5. Which continent is south of Europe and between the Atlantic and Indian oceans?

_____

6. Which continent extends west from the Dardanelles, the Black Sea, and the Ural Mountains?

_____

7. Which continent is the largest?

_____

8. Which continents cross the equator?

_____

9. What continent lies between the South Pacific and South Atlantic oceans?

_____

10. Which continent is basically centered around the South Pole?

_____

11. Which is the smallest continent?

_____

12. Through which continent does the prime meridian run?

_____

Water, Water Everywhere

Blue is usually used to indicate bodies of water. If you look at a globe or a world map, you will see that much of the earth is covered by water. The great body of salt water that covers about 72 percent of the earth's surface is called the ocean.

Look at a world map or a globe to locate the oceans. The main divisions of the ocean are...

The _____ Ocean* and its southern extension.

The _____ Ocean* and its southern extension.

The _____ Ocean* and its southern extension.

The _____ Ocean.

EXTRA: What is the name often given to the very southern portions of the oceans whose names are followed by an asterisk (*) above?

The most southern part of these oceans is sometimes called the _____ Ocean.

The Largest Ocean

Use the clues beneath the puzzle to help you fill in the blanks and solve the puzzle. You may want to refer to a world map to help you!

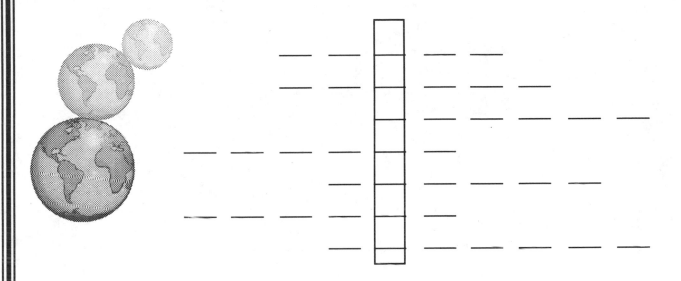

CLUES:

1. This country of Asia is an archipelago, or large group of islands, off the mainland; it is washed on the east by the western Pacific Ocean.

2. This is the only state of the United States of America to border on the Arctic Ocean.

3. This group of Spanish islands in the Atlantic Ocean is off the northwest coast of Africa.

4. This South American country is bordered on the east by the Atlantic Ocean; it is the largest country of South America.

5. This continent is bordered by the Atlantic Ocean on the west and the Indian Ocean on the east.

6. This island state, the fiftieth state to become one of the United States, is in the central Pacific Ocean.

7. This "hot" South American country is bordered on the west by the Pacific Ocean; its capital is Quito.

Write down the letters in the boxed area in the order in which they appear. They will spell the name of the largest ocean.

The _____ Ocean is the largest.

Lakes

Lakes are bodies of fresh or salt water surrounded by land. This map shows the five very large freshwater lakes in North America known as the Great Lakes.

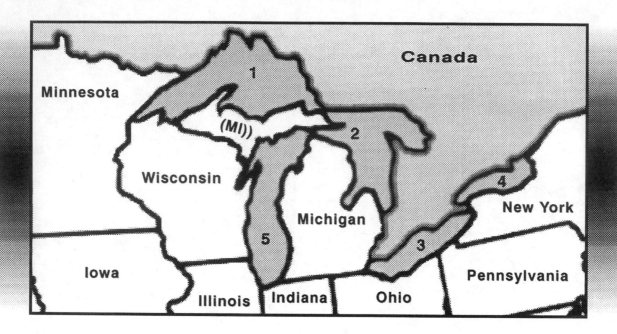

List the names of the Great Lakes. You may use a map of North America to help you.

1. _____   4. _____

2. _____   5. _____

3. _____

Label the map.

The following are other well-known lakes of the world. The continent in which each is located is given in parentheses. Unscramble the letters to figure out the names.

6. C V I R O T I A (Africa)   6. _____

7. E M A D (North America)   7. _____

8. C A C I T I T A (South America)   8. _____

9. R A M A A C I B O (South America)   9. _____

10. A K I Y N A G N A T (Africa)   10. _____

11. I A B K A L (Asia)   11. _____

Scrambled Terms

Use the clues/definitions to help you unscramble these geography terms.

CLUE #1: Land mass entirely surrounded by water.

S I L A D N _____

CLUE #2: A piece of land that projects into a body of water.

N E P N I U S A L _____

CLUE #3: A smooth, usually treeless area of land.

A L P N I _____

CLUE #4: A large inland body of water.

A L E K _____

CLUE #5: A border.

A U O B N Y D R _____

CLUE #6: The body of salt water that covers over 70 percent of the earth's surface.

O E C N A _____

CLUE #7: One of the seven main land masses of the earth.

O C T N I N N E T _____

CLUE #8: A raised, somewhat level stretch of land.

A L P T A E U _____

CLUE #9: A large group of islands.

H C R A I P E L A O G _____

CLUE #10: A list of symbols on a map.

E L E N G D _____

Political Map of the Contiguous United States

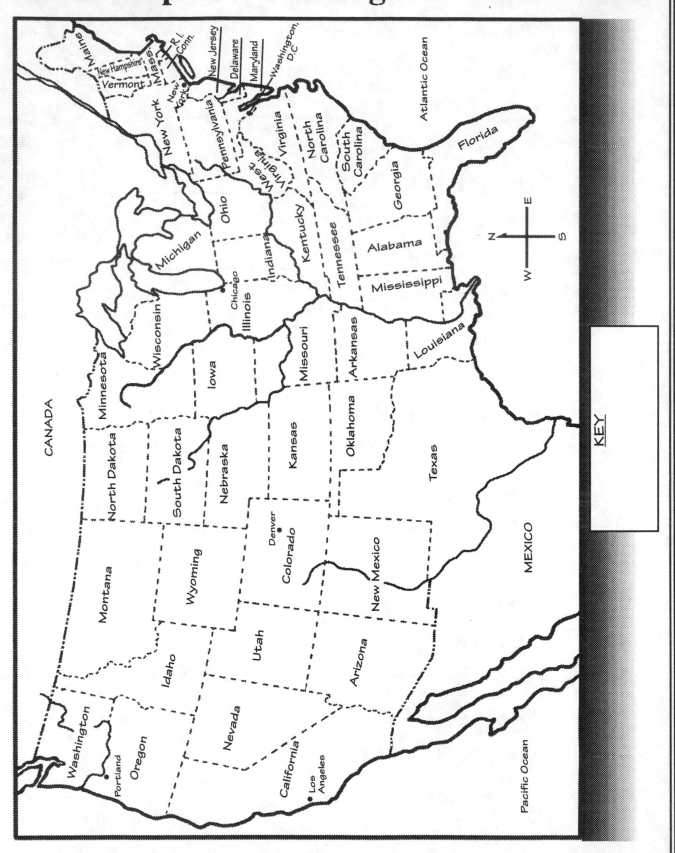

KEY

Dividing Lines

The map on the previous page is a political map. Political maps show political divisions, or boundaries, such as those between states or countries. Although some political boundaries follow natural boundaries, such as rivers or lakes, most political boundaries are artificial—governments agree to where they are.

The map key on the previous page is missing some information. Fill in the blanks.

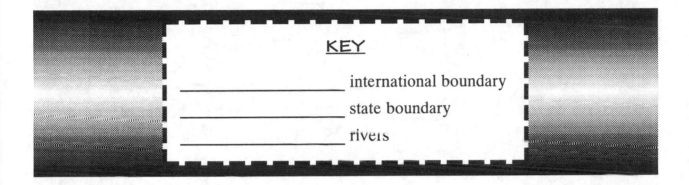

KEY

_____ international boundary

_____ state boundary

_____ rivers

Study the map. Most of the boundaries shown in the map follow imaginary borders decided upon by human beings. Which of the political boundaries shown in the map follow natural borders? See how many you can find.

_____

_____

_____

_____

_____

_____

_____

_____

_____

_____

Stately Questions

This map of the United States of America shows the names and relative sizes of the states.

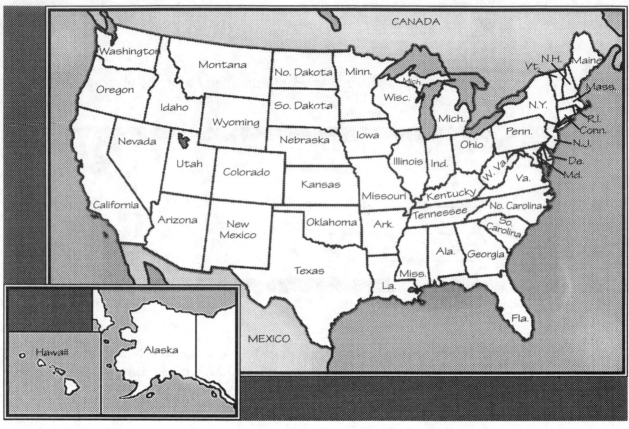

Use the above map to answer the following questions.

1. Which state in the contiguous (sharing an edge or border) United States is the largest?
   _____

2. Which New England state is smaller, Rhode Island or Connecticut? _____

3. The location in the southwest where the boundaries of four states meet is called the Four Corners. Name those states.

   _____

4. Four states have Mexico as their southern border. Name them.

   _____

5. Which state is divided into two parts by one of the Great Lakes? _____

6. Which of the contiguous states is a peninsula? _____

7. Which is larger, Wyoming or Montana? _____

8. Which state is shaped like a boot? _____

9. Is Nebraska north or south of Kansas? _____

10. Which state has a longer north-south distance, Florida or California? _____

11. Which state has a longer east-west distance, Kansas or Missouri? _____

12. Which state is made up of islands? _____

Name the Counties

This map of the New Jersey shows the names and relative sizes of the counties in that state.

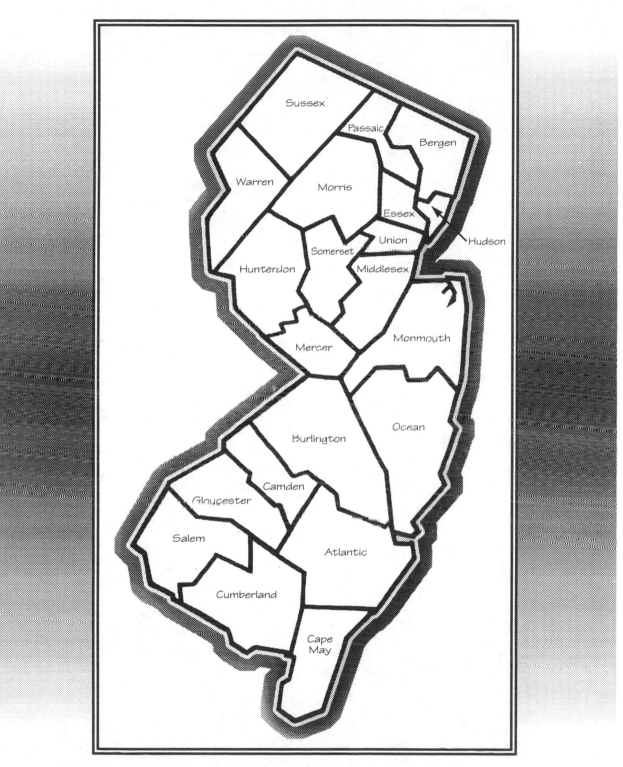

Draw a county (or other divisional) map of the state in which you live.

Agricultural Resources of the United States

Study the following product map.

LEGEND

- — Cattle
- — Citrus
- — Corn
- — Cotton
- — Peanuts
- — Pigs
- — Poultry
- — Rice
- — Sheep
- — Soybeans
- S — Sugar Cane
- — Timber
- ★ — Tobacco
- — Winter Wheat

Where's the Beef?

Use the product map on the previous page and the political map on page 24 to answer the following questions.

1. What crop is grown in Iowa, Kansas, South Dakota, and Wisconsin, as well as other states?
    _____

2. In which state is poultry important, New Mexico or Wisconsin? _____

3. In which state is rice an important crop: Florida or Louisiana? _____

4. In which state are peanuts an important crop, North Carolina or Georgia? _____

5. Find a state that is known for citrus fruits, timber, sheep, and cotton. _____

6. In what other states are citrus fruits important? _____

7. In which of these states are soybeans **not** an important crop: Minnesota, Iowa, Arkansas, Missouri, Illinois, Indiana, or South Carolina? _____

8. Which are more important in Nebraska, pigs or poultry? _____

9. Which are more important in the Dakotas, pigs, poultry, or cattle? _____

10. Find four states where sugar cane is important. _____

Draw a product map of the state or region in which you live.

LEGEND

Population Density of the United States

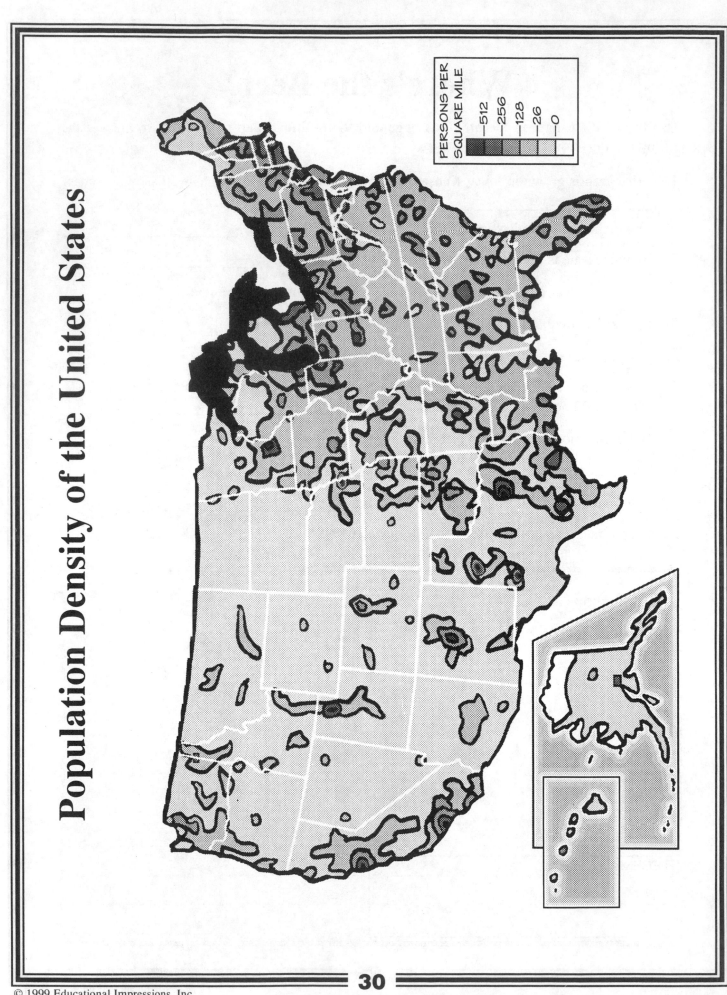

PERSONS PER SQUARE MILE

—512
—256
—128
—26
—0

Where Have All the People Gone?

Study the population map on the previous page. Then answer the following questions about the population density of the United States. (You may have to refer to the political map on page 24.)

1. Which half of the country has a denser population, east or west? _____

2. Which has a denser population, New Jersey or Colorado? _____

3. How many people are there per square mile (kilometer) in most of Alaska? _____

4. Which region has the densest population: the Northeast, the Southeast, the Central Plains, the Southwest, or the Northwest? _____

5. Which city has a denser population, Chicago or Denver? _____

6. Which city has a denser population, Portland or Los Angeles? _____

7. What is the population density of the area in which you live? _____

In the space below, list the pros and cons of living in an area that is densely populated.

LIVING IN A DENSELY POPULATED AREA	
PROS	CONS

If you had your choice, would you rather live in a densely, moderately, or scarcely populated area? Explain.

_____

_____

_____

_____

Create a Map

Create a map of an amusement park, an aquarium, or a zoological park.

Create a symbol for each of the animal groups, rides, shows, etc., that you will be featured in your park. Also include rest rooms, souvenir shops, cafeterias, snack carts, telephones, rest rooms, picnic areas, ticket booths, and any other special areas you want to have in your park.

Be sure to explain the meaning of your symbols in a legend.

Figure out how far apart each exhibit, etc., will be. Create a scale that shows relative distance on your map.

Draw a compass on your map to indicate direction.

Indicate the walking paths. Also show shuttles, monorails, or any other type of transportation that is available within your park. Add these to your legend.

Give your park a name.

Draw your map on the page provided. (Use additional sheets if necessary.)

A Map of _____

A Historical Map

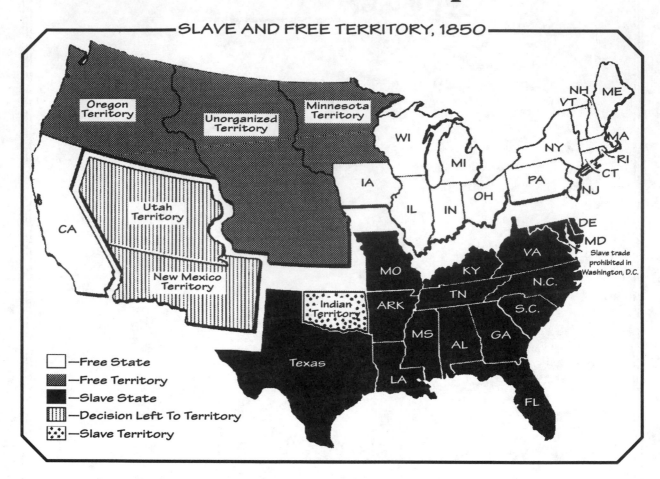

SLAVE AND FREE TERRITORY, 1850

□ —Free State
▓ —Free Territory
■ —Slave State
▥ —Decision Left To Territory
▨ —Slave Territory

The above historical map shows slave and free territories of the United States of America in 1850. Use the map to answer the following questions.

1. Which two territories were to be given a choice as to whether to be slave or free?

_____

2. Which territory was a slave territory?

_____

3. How many states were free states?

_____

4. How many states were slave states?

_____

5. Which territories were free?

_____

Map Projections

Because flat maps cannot really show the world accurately, mapmakers draw different kinds of map projections. Two such projections are the polar projection and the Mercator projection.

POLAR PROJECTION

A polar projection has either the North Pole or the South Pole at its center. Lines of latitude are drawn as circles. Lines of longitude are drawn as straight lines. Where are the distances more accurate?

_____

_____

_____

_____

_____

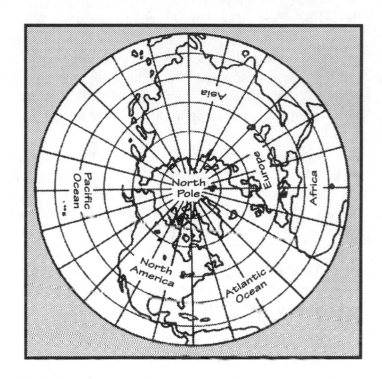

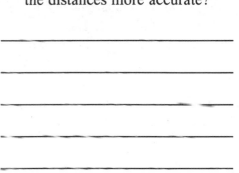

MERCATOR PROJECTION

A Mercator projection shows the lines of latitude and longitude as crossing at right angles. All the lines are straight. Where are the distances more accurate?

_____

_____

_____

_____

_____

Globes

A globe is a model of the earth. Because a globe is round like the earth, it gives us a more accurate picture of what the earth is like than a map does. Globes come in all sizes. Some globes rest in a wooden or metal stand, called a cradle. Others are mounted on a center axis to show how the earth rotates. They are set on a tilt, or slant. That's because Earth itself is tilted on its axis.

Like maps, globes can give us a lot of information about the world in which we live. Political globes show national boundaries; that is, they show the way the world is divided into countries. Often, the coloring on a political globe makes the area of each nation stand out clearly. Capitals and other important cities are also shown.

Physical globes are useful in the study of geography. Sometimes the mountains are raised so that you can feel them with your hands; this type of globe is called a raised-relief globe. Different colors are used to show mountains, valleys, and plateaus. Blue is used to show the oceans, lakes, and rivers. More complicated globes often show warm and cold ocean currents as well.

Like maps, globes also have a scale. For example, on a 12-inch globe, one inch would equal 660 miles; one centimeter would equal 418 kilometers. Globes also have a legend explaining the symbols used on the map.

Imaginary Lines

On a globe you will find many lines. These lines help us to locate places on the earth. Of course, there are really no lines drawn on the earth!

The earth may be divided in half. Each half is called a hemisphere. There are four hemispheres. We can divide the earth into the **Northern Hemisphere** and the **Southern Hemisphere**, or we can divide it into the **Eastern Hemisphere** and the **Western Hemisphere**. If you look at a globe, you will see a line that runs around the middle of the earth. This line is called the equator. The equator divides the earth into the Northern Hemisphere and the Southern Hemisphere. If you look at the globe from pole to pole, you will find another line. This line is called the prime meridian. Many years ago it was agreed upon that this line would pass through a town in England called Greenwich. The prime meridian is used to divide the earth into the Eastern Hemisphere and the Western Hemisphere.

The earth is so large that just dividing it into halves was not enough to make it easy to locate places. People who make maps, called cartographers, decided to divide the globe into sections. They drew lines from the North Pole to the South Pole. These lines are called **lines of longitude**. They are also called meridians. The prime meridian, too, is a line of longitude.

Each line of longitude is given a number of degrees. The symbol used to represent degrees is a small circle (°). The prime meridian is 0°. Each line of longitude shown on a globe is 15 degrees apart. Those east of the prime meridian are referred to as east longitude. Those west of the prime meridian are called lines of west longitude. Lines of east and west longitude meet at the 180° line, or the 180° meridian—halfway around the world from the prime meridian.

Cartographers also drew lines running around the globe from west to east. These lines are called **lines of latitude,** or parallels. The equator is also a line of latitude. On a globe lines of latitude are marked ten, fifteen, or another number of degrees apart. The equator is at 0°. Those north of the equator are called lines of north latitude. Those south of the equator are referred to as lines of south latitude.

Label the following: axis, equator, prime meridian, North Pole, South Pole, Northern Hemisphere, Southern Hemisphere, Eastern Hemisphere, and Western Hemisphere.

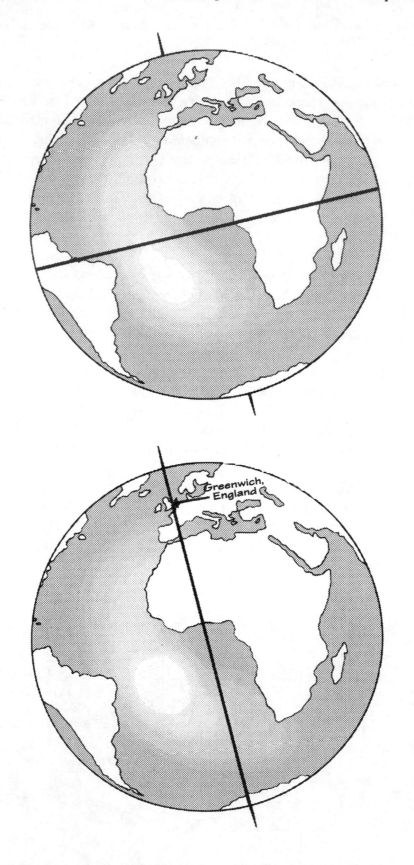

Draw a chart that uses longitude lines to show why a globe gives a truer picture of relative size than does a map.

A great circle is any circle that divides the earth into two equal halves. The shortest distance between two points on the earth or on a globe is called a great circle route. Explain which of the imaginary lines on a globe are great circles.

Study a globe. Look at the northern and southern hemispheres. Determine which is called a land hemisphere and which is called a water hemisphere.

Use a piece of string or a tape measure to measure the distance between meridians, or lines of longitude, on a globe. Measure them at the following locations: the poles, the Arctic Circle, the Antarctic Circle, the Tropic of Cancer, the Tropic of Capricorn, and the equator. Summarize the results of your experiment.

Demonstrate that most of the earth is covered with water. Turn the globe until one side is almost completely covered with water.

Some globes have a metal piece attached to them. Like the lines of longitude, this piece is called a meridian. Find out the purpose of this type of meridian and write a definition.

Longitude and Time Zones

We get our idea of time zones from the sun. The sun shines on the earth and gives it light. Meanwhile, the earth is constantly turning from west to east. Every day—every twenty-four hours—the earth makes one complete turn, or rotation. As the earth turns, one half of the earth is turned toward the sun. It is daytime for that half of the earth. The other half of the earth is turned away from the sun. It is nighttime for that half of the earth.

The earth is divided into time zones. Each time zone takes up about 15 degrees of longitude. That's because as the earth rotates, it moves through 15 degrees of longitude every hour. There are a total of twenty-four time zones—one for each hour of the day. These time zones zigzag so that a city or town isn't divided into two different zones.

When the sun is almost directly over an area, it is 12:00 noon in that area. Because the earth constantly moves from west to east, an hour later the sun will be over the time zone to its west.

New York City is in the Eastern Time Zone. When the sun is directly over New York City and the other places in the Eastern Time Zone, it is 12:00 noon in those places. An hour later the sun will be directly over Chicago, Illinois, and other places in the Central Time Zone. Then it will be 1:00 P.M. in New York City and 12:00 noon in Chicago. An hour later the sun will be directly over Denver, Colorado, and other places in the Mountain Time Zone; it will be 12:00 noon in those places. When it is noon in Denver, it is 1:00 P.M. in Chicago and 2:00 P.M. in New York City.

All the while the earth keeps moving from west to east. Every hour the earth moves another 15 degrees. By the time it is 12:00 noon in Tokyo, Japan, it is 10:00 P.M. in New York City.

With a friend, use a globe to demonstrate day and night. One of you will shine a flashlight on the globe, pretending that the flashlight is the sun and the globe is the earth. The other will slowly rotate the globe from west to east.

World Time Zones

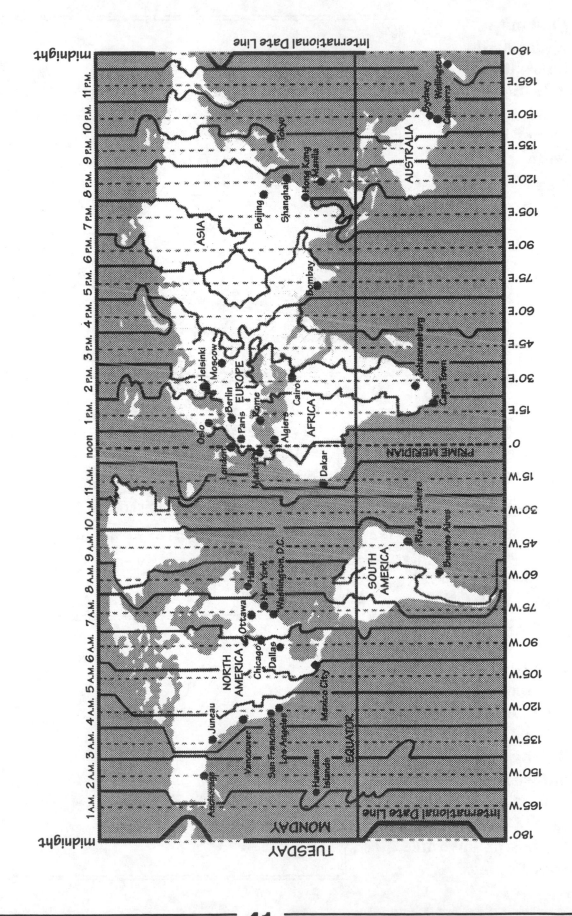

Find out what is meant by the international date line. Create a cartoon whose humor is based on the date line.

Use the World Time Zone chart to figure out the time in the following places when it is noon in London, England:

Dakar, Senegal _____

Washington, D.C. _____

Anchorage, Alaska _____

Bombay, India _____

Rio de Janeiro, Brazil _____

San Francisco, California _____

Canberra, Australia _____

Moscow, Russia _____

Time zones came into being in 1883. Until then people pretty much told time by the sun. It might be 12:00 noon in Town A and 12:10 in nearby Town B. Find out what technology made time zones necessary. Draw a picture in the box to illustrate your findings.

Latitude and Climate

The lines we see on a globe that go from east to west are called lines of latitude. Latitude lines help us to know where a place is.

Just as each line of longitude has a number given in degrees, so does each line of latitude. The line that runs right around the middle of the earth—halfway between the poles—is called the equator. The equator is at zero degrees (0°) latitude. Lines north of the equator are known as north latitude lines. Those south of the equator are called south latitude lines. Latitude lines, both north and south, are also known as parallels.

On this globe, the lines of latitude are marked 10 degrees apart. The line just north of the equator is 10 degrees north latitude, or 10°N. The next lines are 20°N, 30°N, and so on—until we get to 90°N, the number given to the North Pole.

LABEL THE DEGREES NORTH LATITUDE:

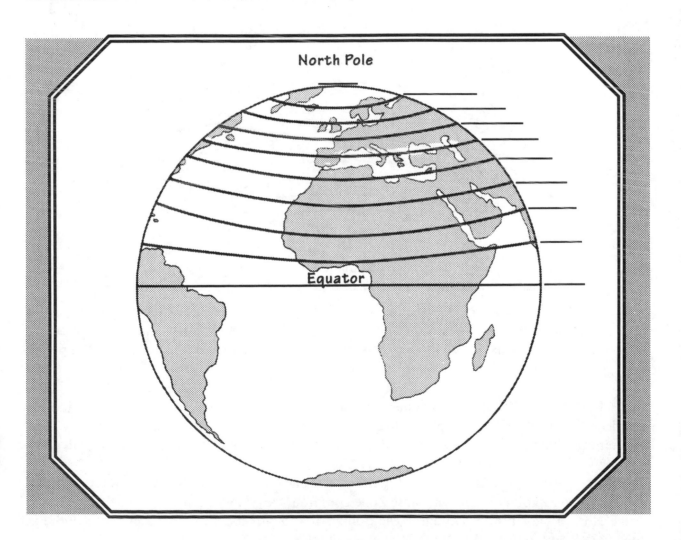

Lines south of the equator run in a similar way. The line just south of the equator is 10 degrees south latitude, or 10°S. The next lines are 20°S, 30°S, and so on—until we get to 90°S, the number given to the South Pole.

LABEL THE DEGREES SOUTH LATITUDE:

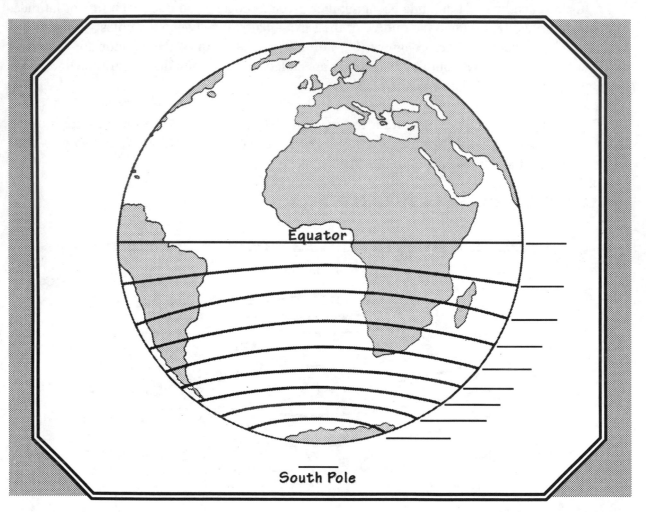

Latitude has a great effect on climate. In fact, it has a greater effect than any other single factor. Climate is the usual weather in an area over a long period of time. Earth is divided into five main climatic belts: the Tropical Zone, the North Temperate Zone, the South Temperate Zone, the North Arctic Zone, and the South Arctic Zone.

The Tropical Zone is the area between two imaginary lines: the Tropic of Cancer and the Tropic of Capricorn. These imaginary lines are at about 23°N and 23°S latitude respectively. The equator is at the middle of this zone. In this region of low latitudes, temperatures are usually hot.

The North Arctic Zone and the South Arctic Zone—the zones of highest latitude—are the areas of extreme cold. The North Arctic Zone goes from the Arctic Circle, at about 67°N latitude, to the North Pole, at 90°N latitude. The South Arctic Zone goes from the Antarctic Circle, at about 67° S latitude, and the South Pole, at about 90°S latitude.

The North Temperate Zone goes from the Tropic of Cancer to another imaginary line called the Arctic Circle. These lines are at 23°N latitude and 67°N latitude respectively. The South Temperate Zone goes from the Tropic of Capricorn south to the Antarctic Circle. These lines are at about 23°S latitude and 67°S latitude respectively. Temperatures in the temperate zones vary greatly, but they seldom have temperatures as extreme as those in the other climatic belts. It is in the areas of middle latitude that most people of the earth live. Here it is easiest to grow food.

Draw an appropriate picture in each box.

Tropical Zone	**Arctic Zone**

Temperate Zone: Autumn	**Temperate Zone: Spring**

The Climatic Zones

Label the five main climatic zones and the imaginary lines that form their borders.

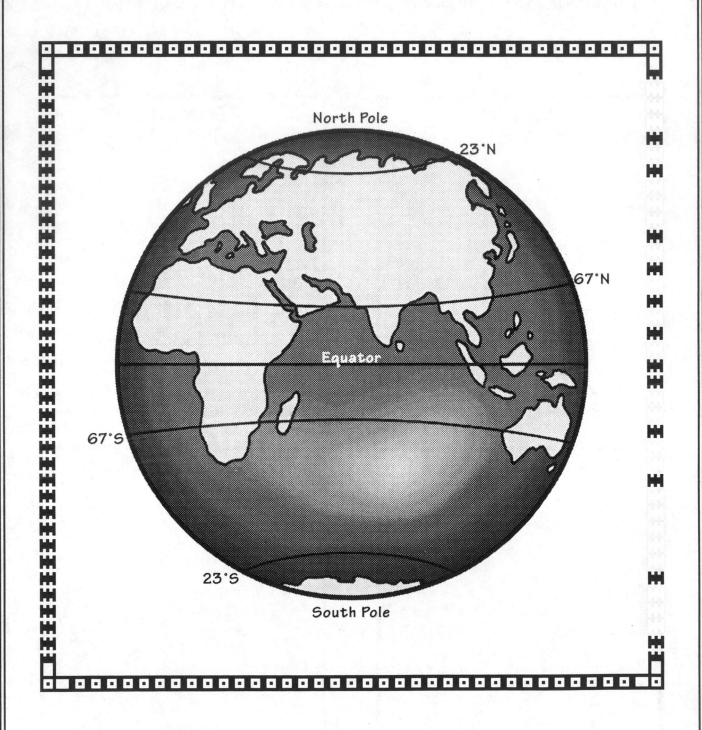

North Pole

23°N

67°N

Equator

67°S

23°S

South Pole

The Seasons

All parts of the earth experience some change in seasons. Near the equator and at the poles the changes are hardly noticeable. The temperate zones—the middle latitude zones—have the greatest changes. In these zones we have four definite seasons: winter; spring; summer; and autumn, or fall.

The seasons change because the earth revolves around the sun. As it travels, its slant toward the sun changes. The part of the earth slanted toward the sun has summer and warmer temperatures. That part gets the sun's rays more directly. The part of the earth slanted away from the sun's rays has winter and colder temperatures. During autumn and spring the earth is slanted neither toward the sun nor away from it.

Regions south of the equator have seasons opposite to those north of the equator. This is because the sun is directly over the Tropic of Capricorn on about December 22, but it is directly over the Tropic of Cancer on about June 21. South of the equator summer begins in December and winter begins in June. North of the equator summer begins in June and winter begins in December.

DECEMBER 22

Latitude also has a lot to do with how wet an area is. Near the equator the air absorbs a lot of moisture from the warm parts of the ocean. Much of the moisture falls on nearby land as rain. That is why many of the wettest places in the world are near the equator.

Latitude has something to do with wind, too. Air heated by the sun expands and rises. Cooler air flows in to take its place. This movement of air is wind.

The great flows of wind are called the prevailing winds. In the areas of low latitude, the winds blow from east to west. In the middle latitudes, they blow west to east.

Latitude is the most important factor in determining climate; however, it is not the only factor. Explain other factors that affect climate.

Look up the word "parallel" in the dictionary. Use a piece of string or a tape measure to demonstrate on a globe why we sometimes refer to lines of latitude as parallels.

Use a piece of string or tape measure to determine what happens to lines of latitude as they get closer to the poles. Summarize your findings.

Write a paragraph describing the climatic region in which you live. Keep in mind the following factors: hemisphere, latitude, mountains, bodies of water, and so on.

Write a list of five cities of the world. Identify them only by their approximate latitude and longitude. Exchange with classmates to solve.

City Match

Match the latitude/longitude description on the left with the city on the right. Use a world map or a globe to help you.

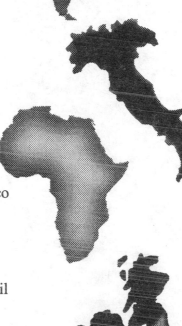

___ 1. 41°N, 74°W   A. Cape Town, South Africa

___ 2. 49°N, 2°E   B. New York, New York

___ 3. 52°N, 0°W   C. Denver, Colorado

___ 4. 42°N, 13°E   D. Quito, Ecuador

___ 5. 34°S, 18°E   E. Paris, France

___ 6. 34°N, 139°E   F. Tokyo, Japan

___ 7. 40°N, 105°W   G. San Juan, Puerto Rico

___ 8. 18°N, 66°W   H. London, England

___ 9. 0°S, 79°W   I. Rio de Janeiro, Brazil

___ 10. 23°S, 43°W   J. Rome, Italy

EXTRA: The prime meridian is neither east nor west longitude. The equator is neither north nor south latitude. Explain why No. 3 is listed as 0°W latitude and No. 9 is listed as 0°S longitude.

_____

_____

_____

_____

North America

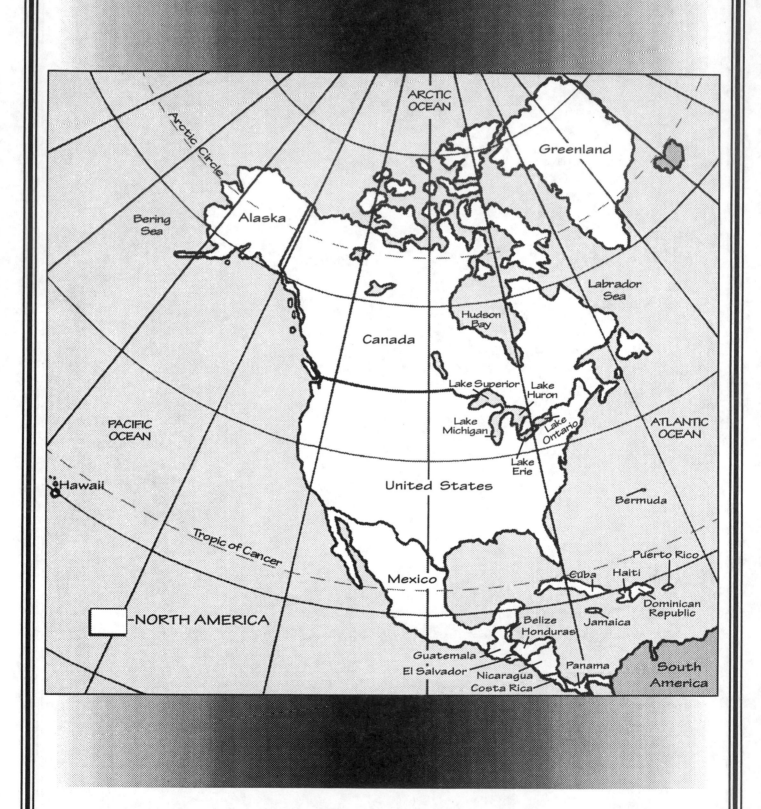

NORTH AMERICA

Using the Map of North America

1. Central America links North and South America. Name the seven nations of Central America.

_____

2. What direction would you travel to go from the United States to Canada?

_____

3. The world's largest island lies northeast of the North American continent. Name it.

_____

4. What body of water borders Alaska on the west?

_____

5. The world's second largest country in area (after Russia) is in North America. Name it.

_____

6. Through which North American country does the Tropic of Cancer run?

_____

7. Name the island nation directly south of Florida.

_____

8. Which is the only state of the U.S.A. to be located on the Arctic Circle?

_____

9. What is the only country to border Canada?

_____

10. Name the bay of the Atlantic Ocean located in E. Central Canada.

_____

South America

CARIBBEAN SEA

NORTH ATLANTIC OCEAN

VENEZUELA

COLOMBIA

GUYANA

FRENCH GUIANA

SURINAME

Equator

ECUADOR

PERU

BRAZIL

BOLIVIA

Tropic of Capricorn

CHILE

PARAGUAY

SOUTH PACIFIC OCEAN

ARGENTINA

URUGUAY

SOUTH ATLANTIC OCEAN

FALKLAND ISLANDS (U.K.)

SOUTH GEORGIA ISLAND (U.K.)

Using the Map of South America

1. What is the largest nation of South America?

_____

2. Which South American nations are crossed by the equator?

_____

3. At which Central American nation is Central America connected to South America?

_____

4. Which country stretches in a narrow strip from Peru to the southern tip of the continent?

_____

5. What are the only landlocked nations (not bordered by an ocean or sea) of South America?

_____

6. What direction would you have to travel to go from Guyana to Suriname?

_____

7. What direction would you have to travel to go from French Guiana to Venezuela?

_____

8. What body of water lies north of Colombia and Venezuela?

_____

9. What is the second largest country of South America?

_____

10. Through which country does the Tropic of Capricorn **not** run: Chile, Argentina, Bolivia, or Paraguay?

_____

Asia

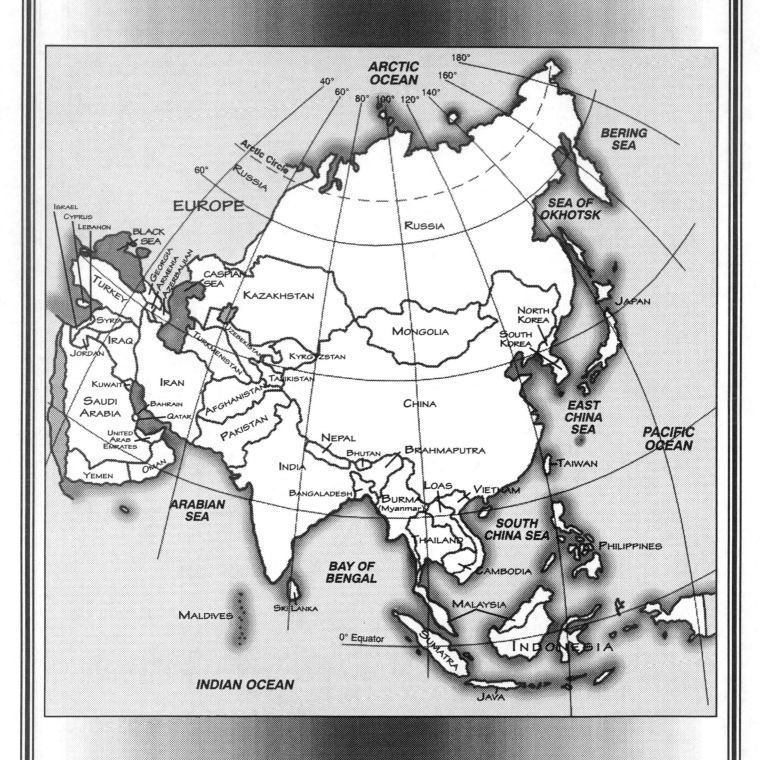

Using the Map of Asia

1. In which two continents is Russia located?

_____

2. What bodies of water border India?

_____

3. Through which Asian country does the Arctic Circle run?

_____

4. Which is farther north, Afghanistan or Pakistan?

_____

5. What country is west of Oman?

_____

6. What line of longitude goes through Mongolia?

_____

7. Describe the location of Sri Lanka relative to India.

_____

8. Which is larger in area, Iraq or Iran?

_____

9. What three countries border Mongolia?

_____

10. Which is farther south, South Korea or Taiwan?

_____

Europe

Using the Map of Europe

1. In what country is the Vatican City, an independent state, located?

_____

2. What country, located both in Asia and Europe, is the largest in the world in area?

_____

3. Which country borders Spain on the west? Together they form the Iberian Peninsula.

_____

4. The Arctic Circle runs through which three Scandinavian countries?

_____

5. Which Mediterranean country is shaped somewhat like a boot?

_____

6. Which country is farther north, Romania or Poland?

_____

7. Which country is bordered on the west only by the Bay of Biscay?

_____

8. Which does not border Russia: Estonia, Latvia, Lithuania, Belaurus, or the Ukraine?

_____

9. What body of water borders Romania and Bulgaria on the east?

_____

10. The capital city of the smallest Scandinavian country is at 56°N, 13°E. Name the country.

_____

Africa

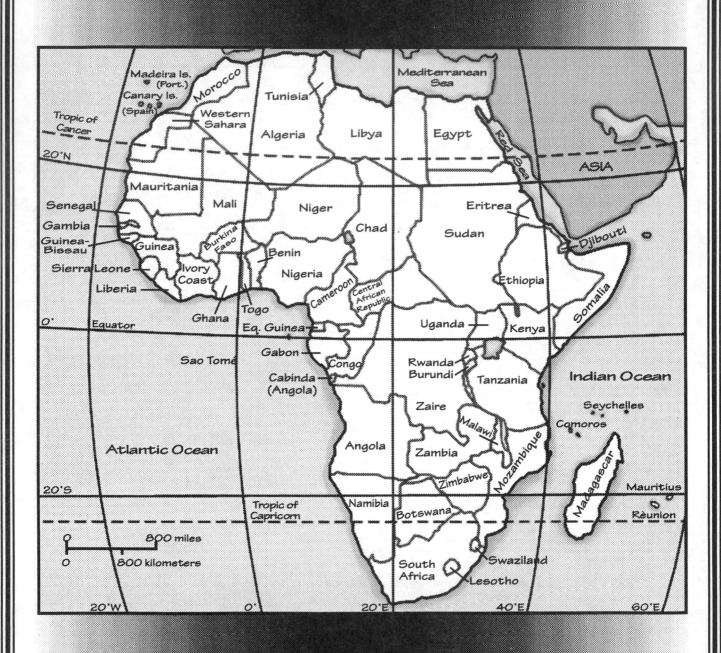

Using the Map of Africa

1. Through which African countries does the equator run?

   _____

2. What borders Tanzania on the east?

   _____

3. What two bodies of water border on Egypt?

   _____

4. What country is at the most southern part of the continent?

   _____

5. Which country is farther north, Zambia or Zimbabwe?

   _____

6. Which country is farther west, Niger or Chad?

   _____

7. Which country is larger in area, Chad or Sudan?

   _____

8. Which island group off the coast of Morocco belongs to Spain?

   _____

9. Which is farther east, Libya or Algeria?

   _____

10. Through which country does the Tropic of Capricorn **not** run: Namibia, Botswana, South Africa, Mozambique, Madagascar, or Zimbabwe?

   _____

Australia

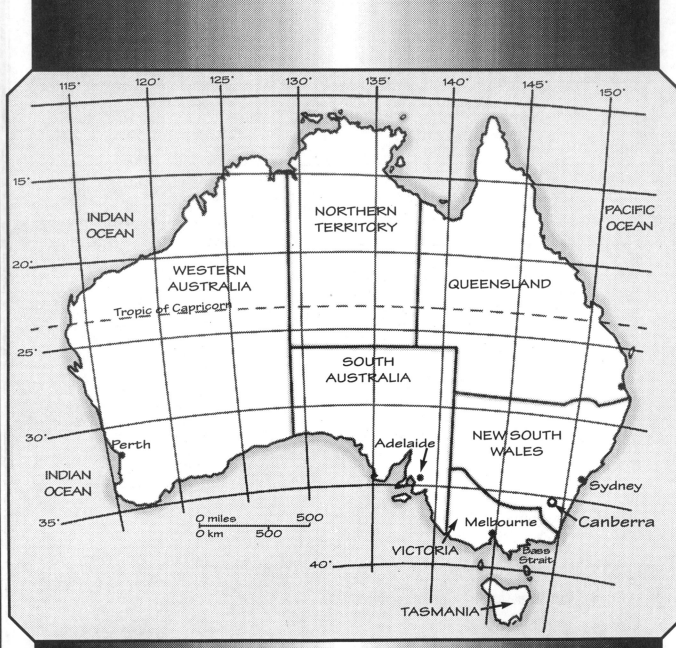

Using the Map of Australia

1. How many nations are on the continent of Australia?

_____

2. What body of water borders Australia on the west and south?

_____

3. Which runs through Australia: the Tropic of Cancer, the Tropic of Capricorn, or the equator?

_____

4. How does Australia compare in size to the the other continents?

_____

5. What body of water bounds Australia on the east?

_____

6. What island is separated from the mainland by the Bass Strait?

_____

7. If the South Pole is at the center of Antarctica, is Australia north or south of Antarctica?

_____

8. Which best describes the mainland of Australia: peninsula, island, or archipelago?

_____

9. In which hemisphere is Australia located, Northern or Southern?

_____

10. Which best describes the location of Canberra, capital of Australia: 40°S latitude, 180°E longitude; 35°S latitude, 149°E longitude; or 35°N latitude, 149°E longitude.

_____

Antarctica

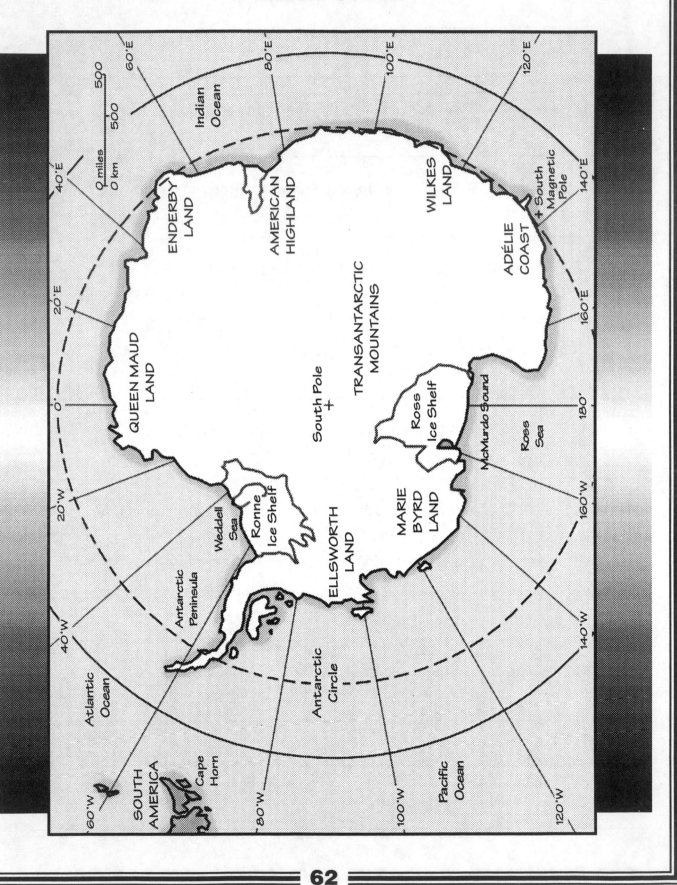

Using the Map of Antarctica

1. What is at the center of Antarctica?

_____

2. Which oceans border Antarctica?

_____

3. Most of the continent falls within which climatic zone?

_____

4. Some of Antarctica's coastline is hidden beneath _____.

_____

5. In which three hemispheres does Antarctica lie?

_____

6. Which longitudes does Antarctica cover?

_____

7. Explain the above answer.

_____

8. Antarctica comprises all lands and waters south of which latitude: 80°S, 60°S, or 40°S?

_____

9. The largest U.S. research station in Antarctica is at the edge of the Ross Ice Shelf, west of Ross Island. Name that sound.

_____

10. What type of projection is this map?

_____

Find It!

Take turns looking for the following things on a globe:

equator	Asia
prime meridian	Africa
cradle, if there is one	Europe
axis	North America
lines of longitude	South America
lines of latitude	Australia
legend	Antarctica
scale	North Pacific Ocean
meridian, if there is one	South Pacific Ocean
Northern Hemisphere	North Atlantic Ocean
Southern Hemisphere	South Atlantic Ocean
Eastern Hemisphere	North Indian Ocean
Western Hemisphere	South Indian Ocean
North Pole	Arctic Ocean
South Pole	boundary lines

Classify It!

Think about the places and terms listed below. Classify, or group, them in many different ways. There must be at least two items to each group. Keep in mind the following when deciding upon your groups: continent, nation, size, location, geographical features, language, spelling, and so on. Stretch your imagination and try to think of some unusual groupings. One group has been started for you. Have fun!

Angola	Ecuador	Mexico
Argentina	Europe	Pacific Ocean
Asia	France	Paraguay
Atlantic Ocean	Greenland	Russia
Australia	Iceland	Saudi Arabia
Brazil	Israel	South America
China	Japan	Spain
Colombia	Kenya	United States
Denmark	Mediterranean Sea	Zaire

IN SOUTHERN HEMISPHERE
Argentina
Australia

Is That So?

Only eight of the following statements are true. Mark each statement true (T) or false (F). Then correct the six false statements.

___1. The prime meridian, which passes through Greenwich, England, is at 0° longitude.

___2. Another word for "longitude" is "parallel."

___3. Each time zone covers about 20° longitude.

___4. Brazil is the largest country in South America.

___5. The equator circles the earth at 0° latitude.

___6. Europe is the largest continent.

___7. Russia is the largest country in the world in area.

___8. Australia is the only single-nation continent.

___9. Africa lies mostly in the Southern Hemisphere.

___10. It is three hours later in California than in New York City.

___11. When it is summer in the Northern Hemisphere, it is winter in the Southern Hemisphere.

___12. Climate has very little to do with latitude.

___13. Spain is south of France.

___14. Kenya is west of Zaire.

Now correct the false statements.

_____

_____

_____

_____

_____

_____

_____

_____

Which Doesn't Belong?

For each set of words, circle the one that does not belong. Then explain your choice. You may want to use a map or a globe to help you.

1. Asia   Brazil   Europe   Africa
_____

2. Canada   China   Norway   Tanzania
_____

3. Madagascar   Iceland   Japan   Thailand
_____

4. Canada   Mexico   Chile   United States
_____

5. Madrid   Vienna   Lisbon   Venice
_____

6. Russia   Canada   China   Luxembourg
_____

7. Hudson River   Mississippi River   Seine River   Ohio River
_____

8. Lake Michigan   Lake Huron   Lake Tanganyika   Lake Superior
_____

9. north   south   under   east
_____

10. Bolivia   Uruguay   Chile   Mexico
_____

11. Zaire   Ukraine   Algeria   Libya
_____

12. Alberta   New Brunswick   Alaska   Prince Edward Island
_____

13. California   Maryland   Georgia   Connecticut
_____

14. Norway   Portugal   Greece   Egypt
_____

15. Japan   India   Ethiopia   China
_____

Map and Globe Word Search

Look in all directions to find the following words. Circle them.

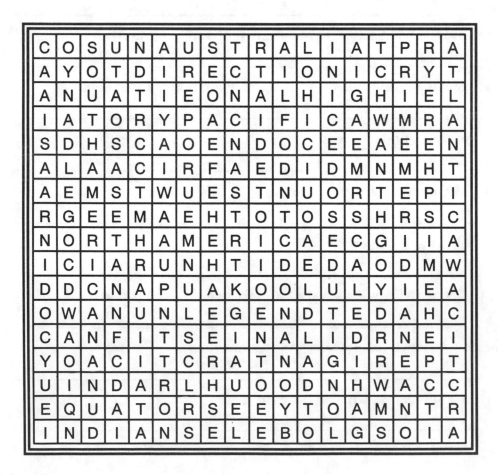

Africa	equator	longitude
Antarctica	Europe	map
Arctic	globe	North America
Asia	hemisphere	Pacific
Atlantic	Indian	prime meridian
Australia	latitude	scale
direction	legend	South America

C	O	S	U	N	A	U	S	T	R	A	L	I	A	T	P	R	A
A	Y	O	T	D	I	R	E	C	T	I	O	N	I	C	R	Y	T
A	N	U	A	T	I	E	O	N	A	L	H	I	G	H	I	E	L
I	A	T	O	R	Y	P	A	C	I	F	I	C	A	W	M	R	A
S	D	H	S	C	A	O	E	N	D	O	C	E	E	A	E	E	N
A	L	A	A	C	I	R	F	A	E	D	I	D	M	N	M	H	T
A	E	M	S	T	W	U	E	S	T	N	U	O	R	T	E	P	I
R	G	E	E	M	A	E	H	T	O	T	O	S	S	H	R	S	C
N	O	R	T	H	A	M	E	R	I	C	A	E	C	G	I	I	A
I	C	I	A	R	U	N	H	T	I	D	E	D	A	O	D	M	W
D	D	C	N	A	P	U	A	K	O	O	L	U	L	Y	I	E	A
O	W	A	N	U	N	L	E	G	E	N	D	T	E	D	A	H	C
C	A	N	F	I	T	S	E	I	N	A	L	I	D	R	N	E	I
Y	O	A	C	I	T	C	R	A	T	N	A	G	I	R	E	P	T
U	I	N	D	A	R	L	H	U	O	O	D	N	H	W	A	C	C
E	Q	U	A	T	O	R	S	E	E	Y	T	O	A	M	N	T	R
I	N	D	I	A	N	S	E	L	E	B	O	L	G	S	O	I	A

A Trip around the World

In this activity you will plan "A Trip with a Latitude!" Choose a latitude. Plan a trip around the world at this latitude. Visit at least five nations. For example, if you choose 20°N, you might visit the following countries: Saudi Arabia, India, Laos, Mexico, and Cuba.

LATITUDE: _____

COUNTRIES TO VISIT:

_____

_____

_____

_____

_____

_____

List at least five sights to see in each nation. These may be palaces, museums, natural wonders, places of historical or political interest, or places of personal interest to you.

Describe how you will travel between nations and within each nation.

What time of year will you travel? What season is it at your latitude? Describe the weather conditions you will likely encounter in each place you visit.

Will you take part in any sporting events? If so, explain.

Draw a picture representing something you will do or see in each country.

Create a travel brochure to entice others to make this "Trip with a Latitude!" Use what you have done in the above activities to help you.

Hidden Places

The cities and countries listed in the box are hidden in the sentences. Find them and circle your answers.

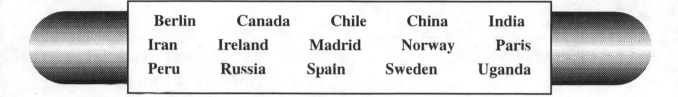

Berlin	Canada	Chile	China	India
Iran	Ireland	Madrid	Norway	Paris
Peru	Russia	Spain	Sweden	Uganda

1. "Can a day go by without rain?" Jane wondered.

2. "If Jane seems mad, ride with me instead," Marge replied.

3. "Russ, I am leaving now," his sister shouted.

4. Every March I leave home to go on vacation.

5. I ran all the way home to tell my mother the good news.

6. Neither I nor Wayne wanted to make the call.

7. "Reach in and pull out a prize from the grab bag," the teacher said.

8. Grandpa rises at 6 o'clock every morning.

9. "Yes, we deny any wrongdoing," the boys stated to the police officers.

10. Linda gave her mother a mug and a vase for her birthday.

11. The baby's pain caused her mother much sadness.

12. Because she was out of tape, Ruth went to the store.

13. A telephone wire landed on the road during the storm.

14. People write about their private thoughts in diaries.

15. In December Linda will visit her grandmother in Florida.

Now create three of your own hidden-places sentences. Hide names of cities and states of the United States. Exchange with classmates to solve your hidden-place sentences.

_____

_____

_____

_____

_____

More Things to Do!

Create three "What Country in the World Am I?" riddles. Use such things as latitude, longitude, direction, and borders as clues.

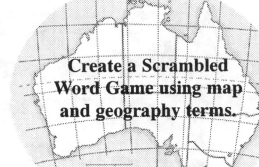

Create a Scrambled Word Game using map and geography terms.

Draw a map to scale of your room at home.

Choose a country of the world. Research that country and draw a specialty map—population density, climatic, regional, product, and so on—of that country.

Create a Geography ABC's. Include continents, oceans, cities, states, countries, and geographical features.

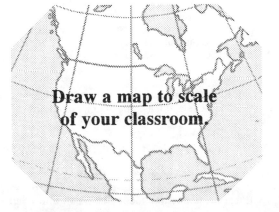

Draw a map to scale of your classroom.

Discovering Maps and Globes
Crossword Puzzle

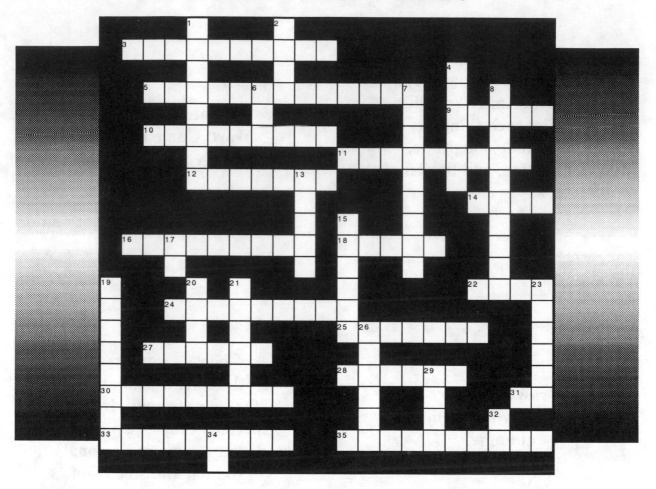

ACROSS

3. Southernmost continent.
5. Used as a reference from which longitude east and west is measured.
9. More realistic representation of Earth than a map.
10. Southern end of Earth's axis of rotation.
11. One of the main land masses of the earth.
12. Imaginary great circle around the earth's surface equidistant from the two poles.
14. A large inland body of fresh or salt water.
16. Only single-nation continent.
18. Shows how distances on a map compare with actual distances.
22. The largest continent.
24. North, for example.
25. What latitude and longitude are measured in.
27. Largest country in South America.
28. Some globes sit in one.
30. The Tropic of ___ represents the southern boundary of the tropical zone.
31. State west of New Jersey. (Postal abbreviation.)
33. Angular distance east and west of prime meridian.
36. Either the northern or the southern half of the earth.

DOWN

1. Angular distance north or south of the equator.
2. Earth is divided into 24 ___ zones.
4. An explanatory list of symbols on a map.
6. A visual representation of an area.
7. The northern end of Earth's axis of rotation.
8. A political map shows these.
13. The entire body of salt water that covers more than 70% of the earth's surface.
15. Land surrounded by water.
17. Abbreviation for southwest.
19. This kind of map might show rivers, lakes, mountains, and forests.
20. Capital of Peru.
21. Country south of the United States.
23. This continent lies south of Europe between the Atlantic and Indian oceans.
26. France, Germany, and Italy are in this continent.
29. This country of southeast Asia is west of Vietnam.
32. Abbreviation for northeast.
34. The Rio Grande separates this state from Mexico. (Postal abbreviation.)

What's the Question?

What's the Question? is similar to the TV show "Jeopardy" in that the information given is in the form of the statement and the student responses are in the form of questions. The questions in Part I are worth 5 points each, and those in Part II are worth 10 points each.

Divide the class into teams of 4 or 5 students. The teacher may act as leader, or you may want to choose a student leader. The leader asks the first group a question from Part I. Whoever raises his or her hand first gets to answer. If the student answers correctly, 5 points are added to the team total. If the student answers incorrectly, 5 points are deducted. If no one wants to answer, the total remains the same. If a team does not give a correct answer, the same question is then asked to the next group. If no group gets it right, the leader gives the correct answer.

When all of the questions from Part I have been completed, the same rules are followed for Part II. The only difference is the number of points each question is worth.

What's the Question?

Part I: 5 points

Imaginary Lines	On a Map or Globe	Geographical Features	Oceans & Seas	Kinds of Maps
1. Goes through Greenwich, England; 0° longitude.	6. Shows how distance on a map compares with actual distance.	11. An inland body of salt or fresh water.	16. North America is bordered on the east by it.	21. Shows us how to drive from one place to another.
2. An imaginary circle around the earth and is an equal distance from each pole.	7. An explanatory listing of the symbols used on a map.	12. Covers over 70% of the earth.	17. The Hawaiian Islands are located in the central part of this ocean.	22. Shows where people live in a particular area, and how many live there.
3. Represents the northern border of the tropical zone.	8. East, west, north, and south.	13. An extensive, level, and usually treeless area of land.	18. East Africa is bordered by it.	23. Type of weather map that shows how much rain, snow, or hail falls in a given area.
4. Represents the southern border of the tropical zone.	9. Political maps show these imaginary divisions between nations, states, or cities.	14. Land surrounded by water.	19. Venezuela's northern border.	24. A book of maps.
5. Used to measure distance in degrees north and south of the equator.	10. Many maps use this to differentiate landforms.	15. Land that projects into a body of water and is connected to main-land by an isthmus.	20. This ocean surrounds the North Pole.	25. Shows agricultural and other natural resources produced in a given area.

What's the Question?

Part II: 10 points

Countries of the Southern Hemisphere	Countries of the Northern Hemisphere	Continents	Capital Cities	Potpourri
1. The only single-nation continent.	6. Its mainland is bordered by Canada to the north.	11. Egypt is located in the northern part of this continent.	16. Capital of Italy.	21. A person who makes maps.
2. The southernmost nation of Africa.	7. Its Yukon Territory borders Alaska.	12. Southernmost continent.	17. Capital of Russia.	22. Used to measure longitude and latitude; they can be divided into minutes and seconds.
3. One of two completely inland nations of South America.	8. These countries comprise Great Britain.	13. Largest continent.	18. Capital of Argentina.	23. Earth is divided into 24 of them, each about 15° longitude.
4. The largest country in South America.	9. Largest country in the world.	14. Russia lies in these two continents.	19. Capital of Kenya.	24. Latitude is an important factor in determining this. Other factors are distance from water, and mountains.
5. Bordered by Chile, Bolivia, Brazil, Colombia, and Ecuador.	10. Three of the seven nations of Central America, which connects the Northern Hemisphere to the Southern.	15. The Gulf of Mexico is in this continent.	20. Capital of Canada.	25. Climatic zone between Arctic Circle and the Tropic of Cancer.

What's the Question?

PART I: (5 points each)

1. What is the prime meridian?
2. What is the equator?
3. What is the Tropic of Cancer?
4. What is the Tropic of Capricorn?
5. What is latitude? (parallels)
6. What is scale?
7. What is a legend? (key)
8. What are the cardinal directions?
9. What are boundaries? (borders)
10. What is color? (raised relief)
11. What is a lake?
12. What is the ocean?
13. What is a plain?
14. What is an island?
15. What is a peninsula?
16. What is the Atlantic Ocean?
17. What is the Pacific Ocean?
18. What is the Indian Ocean?
19. What is the Caribbean Sea?
20. What is the Arctic Ocean?
21. What is a road map? (highway map)
22. What is a population density map?
23. What is a precipitation map?
24. What is an atlas?
25. What is a product map?

PART II: (10 points each)

1. What is Australia?
2. What is South Africa?
3. What are Paraguay or Bolivia?
4. What is Brazil?
5. What is Peru?
6. What is the United States of America?
7. What is Canada?
8. What are England, Scotland and Wales?
9. What is Russia?
10. What are Belize, Guatemala, El Salvador, Honduras, Nicaragua, Costa Rica, or Panama.
11. What is Africa?
12. What is Antarctica?
13. What is Asia?
14. What are Europe and Asia?
15. What is North America?
16. What is Rome?
17. What is Moscow?
18. What is Buenos Aires?
19. What is Nairobi?
20. What is Ottawa?
21. What is a cartographer?
22. What are degrees?
23. What are time zones?
24. What is climate?
25. What is the North Temperate Zone?

Answers and Background Information

Answers are given as appropriate. They are not given for those activities which call for original, creative answers.

Map Match (Page 7)
1. E   2. D   3. H   4. J   5. C   6. K   7. F   8. A   9. G   10. L   11. I   12. B

Fill in the Blanks (Page 8)
1. boundary	2. lake	3. legend	4. cardinal	5. scale	6. globe
7. ocean	8. symbol	9. island	10. plain	11. plateau	12. map

Directions (Page 9)

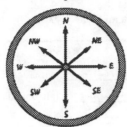

Using Grids (Page 10)
The information is helpful because there is only one square which is both in Column C and Row 3; therefore, there is less area to search.

Scale (Page 11)
Point A and Point B are 2 inches apart; therefore, those two places are 20 miles apart.
Point C and Point D are 1 1/2 inches apart; therefore, the two places are 15 miles apart.
Point A and Point D are 3 1/2 inches apart; therefore, the two places are 35 miles apart.

How Far Away Is It? (Page 12)
1. 6 miles   2. 13 miles   3. 7 miles   4. 10 miles   5. 9 miles   6. 5 miles

Legends (Page 13)
1. C   2. A   3. F   4. E   5. B   6. H   7. D   8. G

C-A-R-T-O-G-A-P-H-E-R (Page 14)
(Be aware that so many words can be formed with these letters that some might be inappropriate for your particular class.) The following words can be formed from the letters in *cartographer:* ace, age, ago, ape, apt, are, art, ate, cap, cape, caper, car, cart, cat, chap, char, charge, charger, chart, chat, chop, coat, cot, crap, crate, crate, crater, crop, ear, eat, gate, gather, get, goat, gopher, gore, got, grace, grape, grate, great, hare, harp, hart, hat, hate, hear, heart, her, hop, hope, hot, oar, oat, ogre, ore, other, pace, pacer, page, pager, par, part, pat, patch, pate, path, pea, pear, peat, pert, pet, pore, port, porter, pot, race, racer, rag, rage, rap, rape, rapt, rat, rate, rater, rather, reap, roar, roe, rope, rot, rote, roter, taco, tag, tap, tape, taper, tar, tare, tarp, tea, tear, the, toe, toga, tore, trace, tracer, and trap.

Road Maps (Page 15)
1. 295   2. 322, 40, 9, 30   3. 45, 49   4. 295, Atlantic City Expressway, New Jersey Turnpike, Garden State Parkway

Weather Maps (Pages 16 and 17)
1. It will be rainy. The expected high is 61°F, and the expected low is 49°F.
2. Phoenix and Orlando are expected to have a high temperature in the 80's.
3. The area northeast of Houston, Texas, to Nashville, Tennessee, is expecting thunderstorms. Snow is expected in Colorado, well west of Denver.
4. Helena, Montana, is expecting a low of 33°F.
5. No, none are expecting ice.
6. A cold front is over the Northwest, headed for Seattle. A stationary front is over the Northern Plains.
7. Boston does not expect rain.
8. Phoenix expects a higher high and a lower low.

Colorful Information (Page 18)
$108 \div 9 = 12$ $6 \times 2 = 12$ $100 - 88 = 12$ $144 \div 12 = 12$ $30 \times 3 = 90$ $45 \times 2 = 90$ $100 - 10 = 90$
$9 \times 6 = 54$ $6 \times 9 = 54$ $54 \div 1 = 54$ $100 - 46 = 54$ $20 + 34 = 54$ $108 \div 9 = 12$ $3 \times 18 = 54$

The Continents (Page 19)
1. No. America	2. Mexico	3. Australia, Antarctica	4. Asia	5. Africa
6. Europe	7. Asia	8. Africa, So. America, Asia	9. So. America	10. Antarctica
11. Australia	12. Europe			

Water, Water Everywhere (Page 20)
The main divisions of the ocean are the Pacific, Atlantic, and Indian oceans and their southern extensions and the Arctic Ocean. The southern portions of those oceans are called the Antarctic Ocean.

The Largest Ocean (Page 21)

1. Japan   2. Alaska   3. Canary   4. Brazil   5. Africa   6. Hawaii   7. Ecuador
The Pacific Ocean is the largest.

Lakes (Page 22)

1. Lake Superior   2. Lake Huron   3. Lake Erie   4. Lake Ontario   5. Lake Michigan
6. Victoria   7. Mead   8. Titicaca   9. Maracaibo   10. Tanganyika   11. Baikal

Scrambled Terms (Page 23)

1. island   2. peninsula   3. plain   4. lake   5. boundary
6. ocean   7. continent   8. plateau   9. archipelago   10. legend

Political Maps (Page 25)

```
                        KEY

 ━━ ▬ ▪▪ ▪▪ ▬     international boundary

 ▬ ▬ ▬ ▬ ▬ ▬      state boundary

 ━━━━━━━━          rivers
```

The following political boundaries follow natural ones: The **Mississippi River** forms the part of the border between Louisiana and Mississippi; Arkansas and Mississippi and Tennessee; Missouri and Kentucky and Illinois; Illinois and Iowa; and Wisconsin and Iowa and part of Minnesota. The **Missouri River** forms the boundary between Missouri and parts of Kansas and Nebraska; Nebraska and Iowa; and part of Nebraska and So. Dakota. The **Rio Grande** forms the border between Texas and Mexico. The **Ohio River** forms the boundary between Kentucky and Illinois, Indiana, and Ohio and between West Virginia and Ohio. The **Columbia River** forms part of the boundary between Washington and Oregon. The **Pacific Ocean** forms the western border of the western states. The **Gulf of Mexico** forms the southeastern border of Texas; the southern border of Louisiana, Mississippi, and Alabama; and the panhandle and western border of Florida. The **Atlantic Ocean** forms the eastern border of the eastern states. The **Great Lakes** form parts of the borders of Minnesota, Wisconsin, Michigan, Illinois, Indiana, Ohio, Pennsylvania, and New York.

Stately Questions (Page 26)

1. Texas   2. Rhode Island   3. Utah, Colorado, Arizona, Mexico   4. California, Arizona, New Mexico, Texas
5. Michigan   6. Florida   7. Montana   8. Louisiana
9. north   10. California   11. Kansas   12. Hawaii

Where's the Beef? (Page 29)

1. corn   2. Wisconsin   3. Louisiana   4. Georgia   5. California
6. Florida, Texas, Arizona, Hawaii   7. Arkansas   8. pigs   9. cattle
10. Louisiana, Mississippi, Florida, Hawaii

Where Have All the People Gone? (Page 31)

1. east   2. New Jersey   3. 26 (10)   4. northeast   5. Chicago   6. Los Angeles

A Historical Map (Page 34)

1. Utah and New Mexico were given the choice.   4. Fifteen states were slave states.
2. Indian Territory was a slave territory.   5. Oregon, Minnesota, & the Unorganized Territory were free.
3. Fifteen states were free states.

Map Projections (Page 35)

In the polar projection the distances are more accurate near the poles. The further away from the poles, the less accurate they become. In the Mercator projection the distances are only accurate near the equator.

Imaginary Lines (Page 39)

On a globe lines of longitude are more narrow, closer together near the poles. On most maps the lines of longitude are the same all over. If you take these narrow, close-together lines and stretch them out, you also stretch out the land within the lines. The lines on the globe, therefore, are more representative of what the earth is really like.

The prime meridian and all the other lines of longitude are great circles. The equator is the only latitude line that is a great circle.

The Northern Hemisphere is called a land hemisphere. The Southern Hemisphere is called a water hemisphere.

The distance between meridians is greatest at the equator. The distance lessens as you near the poles. Because the meridians meet at the poles, there is no space between them there.

The metal piece called a meridian runs around the globe in a great circle. It has the degrees of latitude marked on it to help find a place.

Longitude and Time Zones (Page 43)

The date line, or international date line, is an imaginary line through the Pacific Ocean. It roughly corresponds to 180° longitude. East of the date line the calendar date is one day earlier than to the west of the line. The date line was established by international agreement.

When it is noon in London, it is noon in Dakar; 9 A.M. in Rio de Janeiro; 7 A.M. in Washington, D.C.; 4 A.M. in San Francisco; 2 A.M. in Anchorage; 10 P.M. in Canberra; 5 P.M. in Bombay; and 3 P.M. in Moscow.

The railroads were built. Railroads had schedules to keep. Trains were supposed to arrive in certain towns at certain times. Time zones made the time the same for many miles around. Everyone knew exactly what time it was in every place.

Latitude and Climate (Pages 43 to 48)

Places that are near large bodies of water have cooler summers and warmer winters than places surrounded by land. This is because water turns hot and cold more slowly than land. Ocean currents affect climate; for example, the gulf stream, a flow of warm water that runs through the cold North Atlantic Ocean, warms Great Britain and Ireland. Mountains affect climate. Higher places are colder and wetter. High mountains can block moist air and prevent it from moving inland. Cities are often warmer; sidewalks and building walls hold in some of the heat. Automobiles also make the cities warmer.

To demonstrate why lines of latitude are called parallels, the children can take turns measuring the distance of a line of latitude to the equator. They should measure the same line at several points to show that it is equidistant from the equator as it circles the earth.

Lines of latitude become shorter as they near the poles.

City Match (Page 49)

1. B	2. E	3. H	4. J	5. A
6. F	7. C	8. G	9. D	10. I

The locations given were approximate. The exact reading for London is 51°30'N, 0°10'W; that is why it is listed as west longitude. The exact reading for Quito is 0°13'S, 78°30'W; that is why it is listed as south latitude. For more advanced students you might want to explain that degrees are broken down into 60 minutes. For younger students, simply explain that Quito is slightly south of the equator and that London is slightly west of the prime meridian.

Using the Map of North America (Page 51)

1. Belize, Guatemala, El Salvador, Honduras, Nicaragua, Costa Rica, and Panama.

2. north   3. Greenland   4. Bering Sea   5. Canada   6. Mexico
7. Cuba   8. Alaska   9. U.S.A.   10. Hudson

Using the Map of South America (Page 53)

1. Brazil   2. Ecuador, Colombia, Brazil   3. Panama   4. Chile   5. Paraguay, Bolivia
6. east   7. west   8. Caribbean Sea   9. Argentina   10. Bolivia

Using the Map of Asia (Page 55)

1. Asia & Europe   2. Bay of Bengal, Arabian Sea, Indian Sea   3. Russia   4. Afghanistan
5. Yemen   6. 100°E   7. south   8. Iran   9. Russia, China, Kazakhstan
10. Taiwan

Using the Map of Europe (Page 57)

1. Italy   2. Russia   3. Portugal   4. Norway, Sweden, Finland   5. Italy
6. Poland   7. France   8. Lithuania   9. Black Sea   10. Denmark

Using the Map of Africa (Page 59)

1. Gabon, Congo, Zaire, Uganda, Kenya, Somalia
2. Indian Ocean   3. Red & Mediterranean seas   4. South Africa   5. Zambia   6. Niger
7. Sudan   8. Canary Islands   9. Libya   10. Zimbabwe

Using the Map of Australia (Page 61)

1. Just one. It is a single nation.
2. Indian Ocean   3. Tropic of Capricorn   4. smallest   5. Pacific Ocean   6. Tasmania
7. north   8. island   9. Southern   10. 35°S, 149°E

Using the Map of Antarctica (Page 63)

1. South Pole   2. Atlantic, Pacific & Indian oceans   3. South Arctic (or Frigid) Zone
4. ice   5. Southern, Western, Eastern   6. 180°W to 180°E
7. The lines of longitude converge at the poles.
8. 60°S   9. McMurdo Sound   10. polar projection

Is That So? (Page 66)

1. T   2. F   3. F   4. T   5. T
6. F   7. T   8. T   9. T   10. F
11. T   12. F   13. T   14. F

2. Another word for "latitude" is "parallel."
3. Each time zone is 15° wide.
6. Asia is the largest continent.
10. It is three hours earlier in California than in New York.
12. Latitude is an important factor in climatic conditions.
14. Kenya is east of Zaire.

Which Doesn't Belong? (Page 67)

1. Brazil is not a continent.
2. Tanzania is in the Southern Hemisphere.
3. Thailand is not an island.
4. Chile is not in North America.
5. Venice is not a capital city.
6. Luxembourg is small and the others are large.
7. The Seine River is not in the United States.
8. Lake Tanganyika is not one of the Great Lakes.
9. "Under" is not a cardinal direction.
10. Mexico is not in South America.
11. Ukraine is not in Africa.
12. Alaska is not a Canadian province.
13. California is not on the Atlantic coast.
14. Egypt is not in Europe.
15. Ethiopia is not in Asia.
NOTE: Accept other answers if appropriate.

Map and Globe Word Search (Page 68)

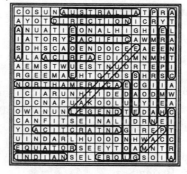

Hidden Places(Page 70)

1. Canada   2. Madrid   3. Russia   4. Chile   5. Iran
6. Norway   7. China   8. Paris   9. Sweden   10. Uganda
11. Spain   12. Peru   13. Ireland   14. India   15. Berlin

Discovering Maps and Globes Crossword Puzzle (Page 72)

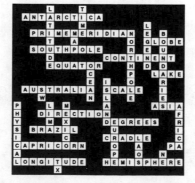